The Rejected Blessing

An Untold Story
of the Early Days
of the Pentecostal Movement

I0164316

Second Edition

by
Jim Kerwin

foreword by
DR. VINSON SYNAN

Finest of the Wheat Publications

The Rejected Blessing

Copyright © 2003, 2012
Jim Kerwin

Scripture quotations marked NASB are taken from the New American Standard Bible®, copyright © 1960, 1962, 1963, 1968, 1971, 1972, 1973, 1975, 1977 by the Lockman Foundation. Used by permission.

ISBN: 978-0-9882667-2-8
(second print edition)

Dedication

For though ye have ten thousand instructors in Christ, yet have ye not many fathers...

1 Corinthians 4:15 KJV

I have enjoyed the great blessing of having *two* "fathers in the Lord." This book is dedicated to the elder of the two, my spiritual father, mentor, teacher, and friend

P.H.P. ("Percy") Gutteridge
(1909-1998)

whose person and preaching first introduced me to the truth of heart-purifying Scriptural holiness.

Holiness by faith in Jesus,
Not by effort of thine own,
Sin's dominion crushed and broken
By the power of grace alone!
God's own holiness within thee,
His own beauty on thy brow;

i i i

This shall be thy pilgrim brightness,
This thy blessèd portion now.

Frances Ridley Havergal
in her hymn
Church of God, Beloved and Chosen

Acknowledgements

Special thanks to...

...Murry Whiteman for the cover design of this second edition:

www.MWArt.net.

...the Larry Martin Collection for photos of Charles Fox Parham and William J. Seymour:

www.azusastreet.org.

...the Flower Pentecostal Heritage Center for permission to use the photo of William H. Durham.

Foreword

IN *THE REJECTED BLESSING*, Jim Kerwin brings to life the first major controversy that divided the Pentecostal Movement after the glory days at Azusa Street. In vivid language, Kerwin almost wistfully laments the fact that the Wesleyan doctrine of entire sanctification as a "second blessing" has by and large become a "rejected blessing" among the majority of Pentecostals. His research reveals the lively and caustic rhetoric of the controversy and the two protagonists in the fray, Charles Fox Parham and William H. Durham.

This story illustrates the general fate of doctrines that are seen in the beginning as a return to Biblical principles and revival, but which are later abandoned and rejected by the movements that created them. Thus the doctrine of an instantaneous, second, perfecting work of sanctification, which was projected by John and Charles Wesley in the eighteenth century, was largely rejected and abandoned by the Methodist Church in the late nineteenth century. After this the Holiness churches that split from Methodism continued to urge seekers to receive the "blessing." The first wave of classical Pentecostal leaders came from Holiness backgrounds and taught the Azusa Street testimony of being "saved, sanctified, and filled with the Holy Ghost." As Kerwin shows, through the "Finished Work" crusade of William Durham in 1911, a majority of Pentecostals rejected the second blessing of crisis sanctification and adopted William Durham's "Finished Work" view.

The Holiness Pentecostal churches that continued to hold to the Wesleyan view did not grow as rapidly as the "Baptistic" Pentecostals, as represented by the Assemblies of God. But in recent decades, there seems to be a growing neglect of a definite teaching on holiness even in these churches. This seems to be the history of most holiness movements. The doctrine is first "projected," then "neglected," and finally "rejected."

Perhaps this fresh look at the unpleasant years of controversy will be of service in calling the Holiness Pentecostals back to their roots and even challenging the entire Body of Christ to look again at the Biblical call to holiness and how it must not be neglected in these days. In fact, many leading scholars are saying that Wesleyans have much to offer the Church in these days of cheap grace and the moral scandals among ministers and priests that have rocked the church in recent months and years.

Dr. Vinson Synan
Dean Emeritus
of the Regent University
School of Divinity

Table of Contents

Dedication..iii

Acknowledgements...v

Foreword...vii

Setting the Stage...3

Two Shifts in Emphasis.......................................15

The Azusa Street Papers and Sanctification....21

So What Changed?...27

A Prophetic Game of Spiritual "Russian
    Roulette"?...41

Why Durham Won...45

True Heirs?..51

Epilogue..63

Bibliography...71

Index..77

About the Author...79

The
Rejected
Blessing

Setting the Stage

AS I WRITE THESE WORDS, the 100th anniversary of the Azusa Street Revival is not far off. In considering the 1906 world-changing outpouring of the Holy Spirit, many scholars and writers, teachers and preachers will be considering "what hath God wrought!" The manifest move of God in that humble church turned warehouse turned stable turned mission at 321 Azusa Street in Los Angeles launched an unstoppable wave of growth: Pentecostals and Charismatics in 2000 (94 years after Azusa Street) numbered almost 524,000,000 worldwide.[1]

---

1   David J. Barrett and Todd M. Johnson, editors, *World Christian Trends AD 30 - AD 2200: Interpreting the Annual Christian Megacensus* (Pasadena, CA: William J. Carey Library, 2001), p. 834. The actual number given for "mid-2000" is 523,767,000. Based on a sustained growth rate of 1.87% per annum, Barrett and Johnson project numbers for the group they label "Pentecostals / Charismatics / Neocharismatics" to reach 543,518,000 by mid-2002 and, if the Lord tarries, 811,522,000 by the year 2025.

As surely as we are human, there is something about the centennial anniversary of this event that will make us want to experience an "Azusa Street" for our generation. We will pray, and study, and consider, and teach, and write, and fast, and seek the face of God. As we do, it is important not to overlook the story of a particular doctrine. Like a faithful handmaiden of the Lord, the blessing of this glorious truth prepared believers' hearts for the coming of the Holy Spirit at Azusa Street. Yet this truth, surprising to say, is hardly known among Pentecostals anymore, for the doctrine became a battleground; the blessing was rejected—the handmaiden cast out. If we don't recover this truth and its heart-preparing blessing, seriously considering its ramifications for our day, we might well miss our generation's Azusa Street. We must seek out the handmaiden and invite her back. Her name is *Entire Sanctification.*

Let us consider the story of how the truth was lost and the handmaiden cast out. In this all-too-true tale I promise larger-than-life (and flawed) men of God, a cherished doctrine violently overthrown, scandalous animosity among Christian brothers, and a contentious prayer challenge in what could be described as a game of spiritual Russian roulette. (The prayer amounted to a death prophecy — which seems to have been fulfilled!) Oh, and just to finish the tale with a strange twist, it will turn out that once the promulgator of the replacement doctrine dies, his followers will promptly change his doctrine to something he wouldn't have recognized, exiling the handmaiden. Let me briefly introduce the main characters in the order of their appearance on the stage of Pentecostal history:

Charles Fox Parham

CHARLES F. PARHAM: This man is credited by most as being at the spearpoint of the modern Pentecostal outpouring. Just after the clock struck midnight, ushering in the first day of the new century (January 1, 1901), Parham and the students at his Topeka Bible College were praying in a Watch Night service. In the weeks previous to the service, they had been studying the Book of Acts and had come to the conclusion that the common denominator each time the Holy Spirit came upon people was the gift of speaking in tongues. One student at this Watch Night service felt the faith to be prayed for to receive the Baptism of the Holy Spirit and this gift of tongues. Parham and the students prayed, and "the fire" fell. In the ensuing days and weeks, Parham and his other students received "their Baptism" and the gift of tongues. Later, Parham's Bible School migrated to Texas, where it would (but almost didn't) enroll its most famous graduate, a man by the name of...

William J. Seymour

WILLIAM J. SEYMOUR: Seymour is, without doubt, the single most-recognized name associated with the beginnings of the Twentieth-Century outpouring of the Holy Spirit. This son of slaves grew up to be a preacher with an overwhelming desire for "more of God." Coming to the conclusion that Parham's teaching about the Baptism in the Holy Spirit and speaking in tongues was indeed biblical, Seymour sought admission to Parham's Bible school in Texas. Whether because of Parham's own personal prejudices (possible) or the prevailing Jim Crow laws[2] in the American South, Seymour, a black man, was admitted to the school with the stipulation that he had to listen to lectures while seated outside the classroom, so as not to mix with the white students. Even though he did not immediately receive the experience of speaking in tongues, Seymour was in complete agreement with Parham's teaching on the Baptism in the Holy Spirit; the two men even preached together in some black churches.

Called in 1906 to preach a series of meetings in Los Angeles, Seymour arrived and taught his new doctrine—only to be given the left boot of fellowship. Locked out by the church which had invited him, Seymour was offered refuge in the home of a kindly Christian couple on Bonnie Brae Street. Seymour shared and prayed, fasted, worshiped and sought God with this family and a few others. Not

2   "Jim Crow" was a pejorative term and a demeaning stereotype used to label Southern blacks (newly freed from slavery) after the American Civil War (1861-1865). Jim Crow laws were discriminatory legal codes, ordinances, and legislation created by Southern whites to effectively disenfranchise, segregate, and marginalize blacks through the Southern American states. Only the passage of federal Civil Rights legislation beginning in the 1960s — one hundred years after the Civil War — signaled the end of the shameful Jim Crow laws.

many days later, first one, then another seeker, then finally Seymour himself received the Baptism in the Holy Spirit with "the evidence of speaking in tongues." Soon the home was too small to host all who came to seek God and "receive their Pentecost." The meetings were then moved to the humble facility at Azusa Street where they were led (if "led" is the proper verb to use of meetings sovereignly directed by God) by this humble man of God. The work brought spiritually hungry Christians from all over the world, and from Azusa Street the word spread back through the nations as the people returned home, and as men and women were sent out from this Mother Church of Pentecost.[3]

Almost as astounding (for its time) as the powerful manifestations of the Holy Spirit in these meetings (which went on day and night for years) was the mixed-race, mixed-gender altar-worker team that ministered to sinners, supplicants, and

---

3   Writer Michael Harper reckons that from the days of the Topeka Bible School until the outbreak at Azusa Street "there were only about a thousand who had received the blessing in the entire United States." See *As at the Beginning: The Twentieth Century Pentecostal Revival* (Plainfield, NJ: Logos International, 1965), p. 19. Comparing this with Barrett's current statistics, it means that the movement experienced a phenomenal 50,000,000% growth in ninety years!

seekers in every meeting. Into these meetings one day in February 1907 came a pastor-evangelist from Chicago by the name of...

William H. Durham

WILLIAM H. DURHAM: I won't say too much about him here, since he gets more treatment when we start our story. At the time our tale opens, Durham, a former Baptist, was pastoring the North Avenue Mission in Chicago. Azusa Street workers arrived in his area preaching the Baptism in the Holy Spirit with the "evidence of speaking in tongues." Once Durham accepted the truth of the teaching, he sought the Baptism diligently, but did not receive it, so he determined to make a pilgrimage to Los Angeles to see the work for himself and to receive this gift of power from on high. What came of that visit will unfold shortly.

I'm tempted to introduce The Cherished Doctrine as another character, the handmaiden named Entire Sanctification, over whom these men fought. Character or not, the teaching still must be characterized, since its place in the story is pivotal. *Sanctification* is the word used to describe the process by which God makes Christian men and women holy, that is, like God Himself. The history and background of this doctrine and its development must be left for a future book, but I can say that the teaching of entire sanctification was crystallized in the ministries of John and Charles Wesley in the 18th Century, and developed by their spiritual progeny (which includes the Methodist Church through its first century, and that denomination's many spin-offs, including the Salvation Army, the American Holiness Movement in the 19th Century, the Church of the Nazarene, the Church of God, the Church of God in Christ, the Pentecostal Holiness Church, and other denominations too numerous to mention). Allow me to give a concise overview of the teaching of entire sanctification:

1. God is holy and He commands His people to be holy, by which He means we are to be set apart for Him alone, and to be made pure in heart and free from sin.

2. God in His grace and power provides the means for us to obey this commandment to holiness, and the means is so thorough that it even destroys or eradicates the inbred sin nature (the "old man," the "carnal nature"). This is where the doctrine takes on its name *"entire,"* since Sin is dealt with at the root. A theological shorthand for this view is the term *eradication.*

3. While being free from the sin nature is important, it in no way implies "instant maturity" or towering spirituality. It leaves the believer for the first time in his life with the ability to not sin (not to be confused with an inability to sin).

4. The most important aspect of entire sanctification is that the heart's ruling passion is the love of God. The "First and Great Commandment" takes on another aspect altogether, that of the Great, Fulfilled Promise: you *shall* love the Lord your God with all your heart.

1 2

5. The Scriptures depict sanctification as both a *process* and an *event*. That is to say, Christians by grace and obedience will grow in holiness, but there is a time when the soul encounters God and wrestles with this matter of inward purity. This is known as a *crisis experience*, that is, a critical juncture in spiritual life when the Holy Spirit, desirous to take the believer deeper and higher in the walk with Christ, convicts the believer of the need for inner purity. When God grants that purity, the time and place are just as knowable and recordable as one's experience of salvation. Hence the word *instantaneous* was associated with the experience, for although there was a process of sanctification leading up to it, and an ongoing process after the event, there was an "instant" when God the Holy Spirit made the heart pure and sin-free.

6. Because this crisis experience is almost always subsequent to a believer's salvation, it was also known by other names, including *the second blessing, the second work of grace,* and even *crisis sanctification.*

The Rejected Blessing

The distillation of this doctrine was the unique contribution of the Wesleys and early Methodism to the Church. With its very personal message, it took root and flourished in rugged, individualistic post-Revolutionary War America, and rode west into the frontier in the hearts of the famous and indefatigable circuit-riding Methodist preachers. Along with salvation preached from rustic pulpits, in brush arbors, and in camp meetings, sanctification was the follow-on message — freedom from indwelling Sin. Thus the teaching of entire sanctification became very much a part of the American spiritual landscape.

Two Shifts in Emphasis

THE TEACHING of entire sanctification evolved over time in two very important ways:

1. One change was understandable—but unfortunate. Most spiritual movements seem to lose their power, distinctives, and even moorings after a generation or two. This appears to happen to any move of God that men touch and try to institutionalize. Methodism and its distinctive doctrine of sanctification were no exception. By the mid-1800s, alarm was growing about the coldness in the movement on both sides of the Atlantic. When reform within the Methodist Church seemed to be failing, many of those who wished to hold faithful to the truth of heart purity left the Methodist Church and formed holiness associations and new churches and denominations. But in ensuing decades of passionate defense of their doctrinal distinctive, some overzealous preachers overstated their case, making a crisis experience of sanctification awfully close to absolutely ne-

cessary for salvation. John Wesley's "remnant of sin" (with which the crisis experience of sanctification was supposed to deal) in a believer had become magnified into "enough sin to damn an entire nation."[4] What to Wesley was a choice between a "higher way" and "lower way" of Christian life became a legalistic demand.[5] It is one

4   Writes William Durham, "Bishop Horner, in his book 'The Root,' makes the astounding statement that a converted person has enough sin in him to damn a nation." *The Pentecostal Testimony*, Vol. 2, No. 2 (May? 1912), p. 3.

5   John Wesley, in the sermon entitled "The More Excellent Way," says: *From long experience and observation I am inclined to think, that whoever finds redemption in the blood of Jesus, whoever is justified, has then the choice of walking in the higher or the lower path. I believe the Holy Spirit at that time sets before him the "more excellent way," and incites him to walk therein; to choose the narrowest path in the narrow way; to aspire after the heights and depths of holiness—after the entire image of God. But if he does not accept this offer, he insensibly declines into the lower order of Christians. He still goes on in what may be called a good way, serving God in his degree, and finds mercy in the close of life, through the blood of the covenant...I would be far from quenching the smoking flax—from discouraging those that serve God in a low degree. But I could not wish them to stop here: I would encourage them to come up higher. Without thundering hell and damnation in their ears, without condemning the way wherein they were, telling them it is the way that leads to destruction, I will endeavor to point out to them what is, in every respect, "a more excellent way."* The Works of John Wesley: Sermons. electronic ed. Albany, Oregon: Ages Software, 2000.

thing to contend for truth; it's quite another to contort it.

2. The other evolution of the doctrine was good—mostly. As the subject of entire sanctification was studied from Scripture and experienced in people's hearts, believers had more appreciation for the role the Holy Spirit played in ministering sanctification to the heart. As a result, the descriptive terminology of the experience of sanctification became more and more equated with the Baptism in the Holy Spirit. This caused more careful study to be given to the Book of Acts and the manifestations of the Holy Spirit therein, increasing the longing in the hearts of the sanctified for a truly, fully Acts-2-Pentecostal experience.

The downside of this linguistic development was that, having been taught that their experience of sanctification was the "Baptism in the Holy Spirit," many believers at the end of the 19th Century had no "theological room" for a fully Acts-2-like experience with the Holy Spirit. Some at first couldn't see how the "new" Baptism in the Holy Spirit could be the Baptism in the Holy Spirit (since it didn't match their understanding of the experience of sanctification styled as the Baptism in the Holy Spirit). Men like Seymour and Parham realized that they had to adjust their theological understanding. Others, who had contended for the truth of sanctification for decades, could not see their way clear to abandon their "Baptism" terminology, and so rejected the new outpouring as "false doctrine."

For these holiness men like Parham and Seymour who could make the leap, the experience of sanctification had to integrate theologically with God's new work. Entire sanctification, as they understood it, had always been "a second work" or second step. The Baptism in the Holy Spirit was now a third step. To them it was perfectly logical that God's *ordo salutis* (i.e., His order or steps of salvation) was:

1. salvation and regeneration, followed by water baptism;

2. a crisis experience of sanctification, in which the believer received a pure heart, free from indwelling sin, thus making the believer a clean vessel, ready to be filled with...

3. the Holy Spirit and power, with tongues and other charismata manifesting themselves.

From this three-step understanding of God's processes in the believer's heart came the very familiar, oft-repeated testimony, "Bless God, I'm saved, sanctified, and filled with the Holy Ghost!"

The Rejected Blessing

The Azusa Street Papers and Sanctification

S O AS IT HAPPENED, "entire sanctification holiness people" were those upon
whom the Spirit first fell in those early
years of the Twentieth Century, and those
through whom the message and blessing were
spread. Like the women at Jesus' tomb, they were
the first ones to bear witness to this wondrous,
powerful, end-time work of God. How is it, then,
that in Pentecostal/charismatic circles today most
of us hear nothing about the blessing of entire
sanctification? How is it that there is so little clear
teaching on the need, power, and ability to be
holy? Why is it that we receive no instruction on
the desire and power of God to make us really and
practically sanctified, to give us hearts that are
pure and free from indwelling sin? This is a part of
our Pentecostal foundation and heritage! Will God
be willing and able to repeat and exceed Azusa
Street in our generation unless we, too, have pure,

clean hearts awaiting a fresh outpouring of the Holy Spirit?

It is an eye-opener to read an intriguing one-of-a-kind book entitled *The Azusa Street Papers*. It contains highly readable, photographically-reproduced, tabloid-sized reprints of *The Apostolic Faith*, the publication of the Apostolic Faith Gospel Mission (a.k.a. the Azusa Street Mission) for the period September 1906 through May 1908.[6] It affords the opportunity to read the words penned by people who were living in the midst of the mightiest outpouring of the Spirit since Pentecost in Jerusalem. It is our heritage, and — especially if we long for a fresh outpouring of God's Spirit in these days — we should know what God did in that humble warehouse in Los Angeles a hundred years ago. Even these nine decades later, the wonder, urgency, and vibrancy of these revival-bred exhortations and reports deeply moved me each time I dipped into the book.

Although "the Baptism of the Holy Spirit" and "speaking in tongues" probably will be the focus of most eager readers of *The Azusa Street Papers*, I

6   William J. Seymour, Editor, *The Azusa Street Papers, A Reprint of The Apostolic Faith Mission Publications, Los Angeles, California (1906-1908)*; Foley, AL: Together in the Harvest Publications, n.d.), ISBN 0-9637090-7-0.

challenge them to do something special while reading. Look for every place where *sanctification* is mentioned. It may be in a teaching, or a doctrinal statement, or a testimony, or reports of what occurred in various meetings or in far-flung outreaches. (Those with a heart for missions will, perhaps, stand amazed at the reports from overseas — Africa, China, India, Scandinavia, to mention a few nations.) If my readers underline *every* mention of sanctification, they will discover what I did: they will have marked *every* page of *every* extant issue of *The Apostolic Faith*! The experience of receiving a pure heart from God as a second definite work of grace in the believer was an almost-universal experience for the tens of thousands touched by God's move at Azusa Street.

Those early Pentecostal saints had a divine certainty in their hearts, based on clear Scripture teaching and their personal, heart-cleansing experience with the Holy God, that the Holy Spirit desired to fill clean vessels, that is, hearts purified by faith. Laying out the doctrinal statement of the church and the movement, the first issue of *The Apostolic Faith*, after making its declaration about justification, said:

Second Work. — Sanctification is the second work of grace and the last work of grace. Sanctification is that act of God's free grace by which He makes us holy. John 17:15,17[7] — 'Sanctify them through Thy truth; Thy word is truth.' 1 Thess. 4:3;[8] 1 Thess. 5:23;[9] Heb. 13:12;[10] Heb. 2:11;[11] Heb. 12:14.[12]

Sanctification is cleansing to make holy.... ***The Baptism with the Holy Ghost is a gift of power upon the sanctified life...***[13] [emphasis mine]

---

7   John 17:15-17 — [15]I pray not that Thou shouldest take them out of the world, but that Thou shouldest keep them from the evil. [16]They are not of the world, even as I am not of the world. [17]Sanctify them through Thy truth: Thy word is truth.

8   1 Thessalonians 4:3 — For this is the will of God, even your sanctification, that ye should abstain from fornication.

9   1 Thessalonians 5:23 — And the very God of peace sanctify you wholly; and I pray God your whole spirit and soul and body be preserved blameless unto the coming of our Lord Jesus Christ.

10   Hebrews 13:12 — Wherefore Jesus also, that he might sanctify the people with his own blood, suffered without the gate.

11   Hebrews 2:11 — For both he that sanctifieth and they who are sanctified are all of one: for which cause he is not ashamed to call them brethren.

12   Hebrews 12:14 — Follow peace with all men, and holiness, without which no man shall see the Lord.

13   *The Apostolic Faith*, September 1906 issue, p. 2, col. 1 (as reproduced in *The Azusa Street Papers*, p. 11, col. 1).

Just so there can be no mistake about what is being declared, on the same page, in the very next column, there is a signed article[14] by William J. Seymour entitled "The Precious Atonement." After first stating that there is forgiveness in the atonement, Azusa Street's pastor goes on to declare:

We receive sanctification through the blood of Jesus. 'Wherefore Jesus also that he might sanctify the people with his own blood, suffered without the gate.' Sanctified from all original sin, we become sons of God. 'For both he that sanctifieth and they who are sanctified are all of one: for which cause he is not ashamed to call them brethren.' Heb. 2:11. (It seems that Jesus would be ashamed to call them brethren if they were not sanctified.) Then you will not be a-shamed to tell men and demons that you are sanctified, and are living a pure and holy life **free from sin**, a life that gives you power over the world, the flesh, and the devil. The devil does not like that kind of testimony. Through this precious atonement, **we have freedom from all sin**, though we are living in this old world, we are permitted to sit in heavenly places in Christ Jesus....

---

14 Note that signed articles were rare in *The Apostolic Faith*, nor was an editor's name ever given. The idea was to bring as little glory and attention to personalities as possible.

> We that are messengers of this precious atonement ought to preach all of it, justification, sanctification, healing, the baptism with the Holy Ghost, and signs following. 'How shall we escape if we neglect so great salvation?' God is now confirming His word by granting signs and wonders to follow the preaching of the full gospel in Los Angeles.[15] [emphases mine]

Even more teaching on sanctification appears on the same page, and more appears in two more columns on the next page of the same issue. And that's just the first issue of *The Apostolic Faith.* I could cite numerous other examples in the other extant issues.

---

15   *The Apostolic Faith,* September 1906, p. 2, col. 2; *The Azusa Street Papers,* p. 11, col. 2.

So What Changed?

S O IF THIS SECOND-BLESSING sanctification was the standard teaching of Azusa Street and all of its far-flung daughter-works around the world, how is it that within six years' time the vast majority of the movement had thrown the sanctification teaching of two centuries overboard in favor of something else? (We'll get to that "something else" shortly.) In part, the change resulted from the fact that more and more seekers came from non-holiness backgrounds, believers with little understanding of the importance (and nuances) of Wesleyan sanctification. But these — and even a good number of "holiness people" — were won away by a most influential agent of change, a man named **William H. Durham** (1873-1912).

As mentioned earlier, Durham was a powerfully charismatic (used in a non-theological sense here!) Chicago-area preacher, who, hearing of the mighty outpouring in Los Angeles, made his way to the humble warehouse on Azusa Street to receive his Holy Ghost baptism. He finally "prayed through" on March 2, 1907. It is ironic (as we shall see) that Durham's testimony appears in the February-March 1907 edition of *The Apostolic Faith* publication, in an article entitled "A Chicago Evangelist's Pentecost." Laying out his spiritual autobiography, as he leads up to recounting his Azusa Street encounter, Durham says,

> Later [i.e., after his salvation] I saw and grasped by faith the truth of sanctification and the Spirit witnessed to my heart that the work was done, and the Holy Ghost wonderfully wrought in my life.[16]

He is, of course, referring to the doctrine of entire sanctification that we have introduced above. He finishes his letter with a powerful testimony to receiving the Holy Spirit at Azusa Street.

Durham's name also appears in a ten-line mini-report about the Pentecostal work in Chicago on page one of the January 1908 edition of *The Apostolic Faith*. There is in this short report what appears to be a completely innocuous, scriptural phrase that would have pleased any evangelical or Pentecostal reader of the publication and elicited many an "Amen": "We have stood by the simple

---

16   *The Apostolic Faith*, February-March 1907, p.4, col. 2; *The Azusa Street Papers*, p. 33, col. 2.

Gospel from the very first, preaching only Jesus Christ and Him crucified."[17] Nothing raised a red flag at the time, not even to Jennie Moore, whose eye-witness account of the ministry in Chicago follows in the very next paragraph of the same issue. (Jennie, one of the first people to receive the baptism of the Holy Spirit in Los Angeles, had become a "first string player" on the Azusa Street ministry team, and was to become Mrs. William J. Seymour less than four months later.)

Nevertheless, that phrase "preaching only Jesus Christ" may have been a Freudian slip on the part of Durham. Pastor Thomas George Farkas, in his doctoral dissertation on Durham's life and ministry, says,

> Immediately after Durham's Pentecostal Baptism at Azusa Street in February 1907,[18] he ceased preaching the doctrine of crisis sanctification: "From the day the Holy Spirit fell on me

---

17 *The Apostolic Faith*, January 1908, p.1, col. 2; *The Azusa Street Papers*, p. 58, col. 2. Durham is employing, of course, the closing words of 1 Corinthians 2:2, to wit, "For I determined not to know anything among you, save Jesus Christ, and Him crucified."

18 This appears to conflict with the date already given (March 2nd), but Durham arrived at Azusa Street in late February and was almost a week in coming through to his "Pentecost." [Note: This is my footnote added to the Farkas quote.]

and filled me I could never preach the second work theory again." He still held to it in theory but could not publicly proclaim it any longer.[19]

Indeed, not only was Durham no longer preaching sanctification as a second work, he was formulating a new and distinctive view of sanctification. And while he was formulating his doctrine, he was very busy and very successful. In the two years between his 1908 report in *The Apostolic Faith* and 1910, Durham formed his own ministerial association so that he could provide ministerial credentials from his Chicago church. His meetings were so well attended that his North Avenue Mission became known as the "Azusa Street of the Midwest." And he became almost the *de facto* leader of the Pentecostal movement when misfortune hit two other leaders. First, Charles Parham's ministry was rocked by public scandal. Then one of William Seymour's most-trusted Azusa Street workers, the ministry's editor, made off with the national and international mailing lists of *The Apostolic Faith* publication, setting up her own publication (with the purloined mailing list — still call-

19 Thomas George Farkas, *William H. Durham and the Sanctification Controversy in Early American Pentecostalism, 1906-1916*; (doctoral dissertation: The Southern Baptist Theological Seminary, 1993), p. 134.

ing it *The Apostolic Faith!*) in Portland, Oregon.[20] Without the mailing list, no Seymour-authorized copies of the Azusa Street organ went forth any more; and without the continuing spread of news about the work, attendance fell off and the famed Los Angeles work fell into decline.

With Parham's and Seymour's stars suddenly dimming, the popular preacher and pulpit prodigy of Chicago became the brightest star in the Pentecostal firmament. As his influence and reputation grew, he prepared himself for his great declaration. Seeing his opportunity at a Pentecostal conference in May 1910, he publicly proclaimed his new view of sanctification in a message entitled "The Finished Work of Calvary." The bomb was dropped, creating a furor and firestorm that eventually resulted in the first doctrinal split in the fledgling Pentecostal Movement.

---

20 This fascinating story falls outside the bounds of this book, but it is given a highly readable and enjoyable treatment by Edith L. Blumhofer and Grant Wacker in "Who Edited the Azusa Mission's *Apostolic Faith?*" This article appeared on pp. 15-21 of *Assemblies of God Heritage*, Vol. 21, No. 2, Summer 2001. Who is the guilty sister? I've hidden the answer somewhere in the bibliography. (How else am I going to persuade you to read through the book list at the end?)

Durham's teaching, which quickly gained the name "The Finished Work," can be summarized in this way:

1. He alleged that there is no Scriptural basis for a "two-step" experience (i.e., justification and regeneration, followed by a separate experience of sanctification) leading up to Spirit baptism. Everything—forgiveness, salvation, new birth, and sanctification come to Christians in the atonement, the single "finished work" of Christ.

2. In that finished work, the "old man" was crucified, and Sin was eradicated from the believer's heart. (This is an important point to which we will return later.) In other words, sanctification was immediate and contemporaneous with regeneration. The Christian received everything at the same time.

3. From regeneration moving forward, then, sanctification was progressive, that is, the believer could grow in grace, maturity, and the fruit of the Spirit.

4. Only the Baptism of the Holy Spirit (as Pentecostals understood the phrase) came as a subsequent experience.

It seems ludicrous on the face of it that Durham could and did express surprise over the furor caused by his teaching, and yet so he claimed in print:

> I never thought this blessed teaching would cause a division among the real people of God. It had never occurred to me that it would be made a test of fellowship, one way or the other. I simply saw that it was one of the most glorious truths that God...had revealed to man...and proclaimed it without considering what the consequences would be.[21]

This certainly seems to run counter to other things that he wrote, including the following:

> When the truth of the "Finished Work of Christ" was first sounded forth through PENTECOSTAL TESTIMONY,[22] a large number saw what a

---

21 William Durham in the article "The Great Battle of Nineteen Eleven" in his publication *Pentecostal Testimony*, vol. 2, number 6 (January 1912); quoted in Farkas, *William H. Durham*, p. 144.

22 *Pentecostal Testimony* was the publication of Durham's ministry, as *The Apostolic Faith* was associated with the Azusa Street ministry. (I am very grateful to the faithful servant-archivists at the Flower Pentecostal Heritage Center for providing me with photocopies of extant copies of *Pentecostal Testimony* and other Durham publications.) By the way, just to keep you on your toes, the publication of Parham's entirely separate ministry was also called *The Apostolic Faith*.

conflict it would cause. None saw it clearer than the editor who wrote the articles on the subject. How could it be otherwise?[23]

As Durham spread the word through *Pentecostal Testimony*, 1910's initial brouhaha and bellicosity burgeoned into battle in 1911. Indeed, Durham referred to the heated controversy as "The Battle of Nineteen Eleven." His attacks on Wesleyan holiness were "stubborn and aggressive,"[24] and his writings carried "vituperation,"[25] hardly what one would expect from a man whose heart was sanctified and full of God's love, at whatever time and in whatever order that sanctification was supposed to occur! (To be fair, many responses from some of his second-blessing detractors and opponents were less than "sanctified" as well.) In 1911 he hit the

---

23 Durham in "The Finished Work of Calvary—It Makes Plain the Great Work of Redemption," *Pentecostal Testimony*, Vol. 2, No. 2 (May 1912?). Note: the ALL-CAPs title in the text is presented as it was in the original.

24 Blumhofer, *The Assemblies of God: A Popular History*. (Springfield, MO: Radiant Books [Gospel Publishing House], 1985), p. 43.

25 William W. Menzies, "The Non-Wesleyan Origins of the Pentecostal Movement," pp. 81-98 in *Aspects of Pentecostal-Charismatic Origins*, Vinson Synan, ed.; (Plainfield, NJ: Logos International, 1975), p. 92.

road, preaching his doctrine at revivals and camp meetings.

Durham visited Los Angeles in the spring of 1911. He was turned away from meetings that had been arranged for him at the Upper Room Mission, because that group's pastor learned that Durham intended to teach the Finished Work doctrine, and he refused to receive him. William Seymour, however, was away preaching in the East, so Durham turned to the Azusa Street congregation (by this time a very small group) and the people there welcomed him. Using Seymour's pulpit, Durham night after night inveighed against crisis sanctification, a doctrine dear to Seymour's heart. Though the meetings were well-attended and very successful, the "new doctrine" troubled Seymour's elders, and they summoned Seymour back to Los Angeles to deal with the crisis. Seymour, on his return, asked Durham to stop preaching the Finished Work doctrine at Azusa Street.

It is just here that Durham's *chutzpah* (some would say *arrogance*) seemed to scale new heights: Durham tried to stop Seymour, the man under whose ministry he had received the Baptism in the Holy Spirit, from preaching in his own pulpit! I'll let Pentecostal researcher Larry Martin tell this part of the story his way:

> Instead of submitting to the pastor of the local assembly, Durham went before the congregation on Sunday morning and asked the people to vote on whether they wanted him to continue the work or turn it back to Seymour. Durham said only "ten or less" voted with Seymour. How Durham could have participated in this unethical and egotistical spiritual *coup d'état* is unimaginable.[26]

Feeling that he had no other recourse in the face of such ungrateful and unbecoming conduct (I almost said bald-faced usurpation), Seymour padlocked the doors to the Azusa Street Mission on May 2nd.[27] Durham's spin on Seymour's action is an eye-opener:

26　Larry Martin, *The Life and Ministry of William J. Seymour and a History of the Azusa Street Revival* (Joplin, MO: Christian Life Books), pp. 287-288. This book is the first of a multi-volume series called *The Complete Azusa Street Library*.

27　In one of those truth-is-stranger-than-fiction ironies of history, Pentecostal-history buffs will remember that after Seymour's first meeting in Los Angeles, the church that invited him to speak rejected his teaching on the Baptism in the Holy Spirit and speaking in tongues — and they padlocked the door on *him!* Perhaps it was a case of "coming full circle."

...while we were preaching, praying, and seeking God in the Mission, Seymour had been scheming and planning as to how he could get possession of the building...[28]

Martin ponders the irony of Durham's interpretation of this lockout:

How unfortunate that Seymour would be accused of "scheming" to regain control of his own pulpit after his pastoral authority had been usurped by a former friend.[29]

Durham even managed to drag race into the issue:

When we came to the Mission Tuesday, we found that Seymour had influenced a few of the officers of the Mission, ***men of his own color***, to stand with him, and they had locked and bolted the door.[30] [emphasis mine]

---

28   Durham, "The Great Revival at Azusa Street Mission — How It Began and How It Ended," in *Pentecostal Testimony*, Vol. 1, No. 8 [some time in 1911; dates are never given for *Pentecostal Testimony*, except for the very first issue]. By the way, "The Great Revival at Azusa Street" about which Durham writes is *not* the 1906 outpouring everyone else thinks of as the "great revival"; instead it was Durham's description of his own meetings at Azusa Street in 1911!

29   Martin, *Life and Ministry of William J. Seymour*, p. 288.

30   Durham, "The Great Revival," p. 4.

Durham rented space elsewhere in Los Angeles and, taking many Azusa Street members and even a few leaders with him, he continued his meetings in town. The meetings were well-attended and much blessing was reported. Durham actually moved his ministry headquarters from Chicago to Los Angeles during this period.[31]

---

31 Parham, ever the opponent of Durham and "Durhamism," took an uncharitable (and, one hopes, untrue) swipe at his deceased nemesis in the December 1912 issue of his *The Apostolic Faith* periodical. In an article entitled "Free-Love," he says, "The man who lately wrought such havoc among Apostolic [i.e., Pentecostal] people by a denial of a definite work of grace in sanctification, either fostered or was ignorant of the fact that free-love had so far permeated his work in Chicago, that some of his leading workers were sent to a certain Home in a delicate condition [that is, pregnant out of wedlock]. This compelled the leader to make his headquarters in Los Angeles for a time...." See page 5 in that issue. Could this have been true? My verdict must be "nay," since I have only Parham's accusation and no corroboration (1 Timothy 5:19). True, Parham had many contacts in the Chicago area because of his ministry trips associated with Dowie's Zion City. On the other hand, an enemy of sanctification (as Parham saw Durham) was easy to suspect of any sort of ungodliness. And obvious distortion (along with unalloyed racial bias) assaults the modern-day reader on the previous page of this same article where Parham inveighs against the "Horrible, awful shame!" of mixed-race, mixed-gender ministry at Azusa Street, another "evidence" in his mind that "free-love" also prevailed in Seymour's work.

But Durham didn't seem to be content to leave injury unaccompanied by insult, so in his *Pentecostal Testimony* he berated Seymour and his ministry:

> ...God had shown me the truth concerning him. He does not care in the least for the work of the Lord...the power of God had left him entirely... he was no longer worthy of the confidence and respect of the saints...I have been the last of all the brethren...to give him up, and have always found an excuse for his failures and blunders... The circumstances have forced this most unpleasant duty on me.[32]

In other words, Durham was telling his large readership that Seymour was a washed-up has-been spiritually and ministerially. This is the same William Seymour of whom Durham had gushed only four years earlier:

> Now just a word concerning Bro. Seymour, who is the leader of the movement under God: He is the meekest man I ever met. He walks and talks with God. His power is in his weakness. He seems to be as simple-hearted as a little child, and at the same time is so filled with God that you feel the love and power every time you get near him.[33]

---

32 Durham, "The Great Revival," p. 4.

33 *The Apostolic Faith*, February-March 1907, p.4, col. 3; *The*

Even some of Durham's staunchest supporters found that the tenor of his anti-second-blessing tirades made them uncomfortable. Frank Bartleman, an itinerant evangelist most remembered by us today as the chronicler of the Azusa Street Revival, found he had reached his limit, though he still admired Durham's public ministry and results.

> I left [Durham's] platform finally, not willing to stand for a spirit of retaliation. I felt I must keep clear of carnal strife and controversy...his word was coming to be almost law in the Pentecostal missions, even as far as the Atlantic Coast. Too much power is unsafe for any one man. The paper he instituted in connection with his work[34] began to take on the nature of a carnal controversy, fighting the old "second work of grace" theory. This spirit the Lord showed me He was about to stop.[35]

Azusa Street Papers, p. 33, col. 3.

34   That is, *Pentecostal Testimony*, from which we have been quoting.

35   Frank Bartleman, *Another Wave Rolls In* (formerly, *What Really Happened at Azusa Street*), edited by John Walker, revised and enlarged edition; (Monroeville, PA: Whitaker Books, 1962), pp. 109-110.

A Prophetic Game of
Spiritual "Russian Roulette"?

PPARENTLY THE LORD was show-
ing people in the opposition camp the
same thing. As the rancor escalated,
Pentecostal veteran Charles Fox Parham (who never wavered from his unflinching
support of second-blessing sanctification) weighed
into the fray in early January 1912. He prayed a
remarkably rash — and (as it turned out) prophetic
— prayer.

> "If this man's doctrine is true, let my life go out
> to prove it; but if our teaching on a definite
> grace of sanctification is true, let his life pay the
> forfeit."[36]

---

36 Edith Waldvogel Blumhofer, *The Assemblies of God: A Popular
    History* (Springfield, MO: Radiant Books/Gospel Publishing
    House, 1985), p. 43.

This type of prophet vs. prophet showdown isn't completely
unprecedented in Scripture. In fact, two Old Testament scripture passages come to mind. The more well-known of the two
is Elijah on Mt. Carmel (1 Kings 18:17-40) when the Tishbite
challenged, "How long halt ye between two opinions?...the

In the June 1912 edition of his publication *The Apostolic Faith*, Parham declared:

> Durham, of Chicago, is now riding blindly to his fall. I want to say as a messenger of God, and the senior preacher of the Movement, that all men who seek leadership in this work and assume the power that alone belongs to the Messenger of the Covenant — the Holy Ghost, will fall...[37]

Friend or foe, it must have caught everyone off guard when Durham — in the prime of his life and just shy of his fortieth birthday — died suddenly on July 7th of that same year. Says James R. Goff, Jr., one of Parham's biographers, "Parham felt that

---

God that answereth by fire, let Him be God." (vv. 21, 24). By day's end, 450 false prophets had met their doom. Then there is the story in Jeremiah 28 about the opposition the false prophet Hananiah made against Jeremiah's word from God. God spoke through Jeremiah, telling him that He would kill Hananiah "this year" (v. 16), and Hananiah died later that same year (v. 17). As sobering and unpopular as the thought may be, God is not adverse to taking the life of one who opposes Him (even in the New Testament, as witnessed by the sad story of Peter's prophetic pronouncements against Ananias and Sapphira in Acts 5:1-11).

37 Charles F. Parham, *The Apostolic Faith* [Baxter Springs, Kansas], Vol. 1, No. 4, June 1912, pp. 8-9. Whether by popular demand or (one is tempted to think of this as more likely) as a "See, I told you so!" Parham reprinted this article in its entirety in Vol. 2, No. 7 (September 1913) on pp. 9-10.

God had properly answered his prayer."[38] Foes of Durham and his "Finished Work" teaching were sobered, no doubt, but rejoiced because they felt their cause and doctrine were exonerated and vindicated. Durham's supporters, if they gave the timing of Durham's death any thought at all, didn't admit to seeing anything ominous in it. They gave him a memorial service with glowing eulogies and ample tributes.

---

38   James R. Goff, Jr., *Fields White unto Harvest: Charles F. Parham and the Missionary Origins of Pentecostalism* (Fayetteville, AR: The University of Arkansas Press, 1988), p. 152. Another of Parham's biographers, his wife Sarah E. Parham, makes no mention of this. However, detailing as she does Parham's itinerations, it is interesting to note that she places him in Perris, CA (not far from Los Angeles) from early December 1911 until January 31, 1912 (at which time he began preaching a series of meetings in L.A. proper). This means that Parham had ample opportunity to hear first-hand accounts of the swath Durham had cut through the Pentecostal community in Southern California the previous spring and summer. This may account for the January 1912 timeframe of Parham's remarkable prayer. *Cf.* Sarah E. Parham, *The Life of Charles F. Parham, Founder of the Apostolic Faith Movement* (New York: Garland Publishing, Inc., 1985), pp. 237-239.

The Rejected Blessing

Why Durham Won

IF THE "LOSERS" in this grand theological dispute had written Durham's epitaph, it might have sounded like the words of Charles Parham (but one would hope that someone would have been more gracious!):

> The diabolical end and purpose of his Satanic majesty, in perpetuating Durhamism on the world, in repudiating sanctification as a definite work of grace, has now clearly been revealed. By seeking to destroy the grace of sanctification he is seeking to efface the only grace of God to make us overcomers, and thereby hinder necessary preparation for Redemption. Let all who have been deceived thereby humble themselves and seek restoration to "this grace wherein we stand" (Romans 5:2), as you cannot receive the real Pentecost on an unsanctified life.[39]

---

39 Charles Parham, *The Everlasting Gospel* (n.p., n.d), p. 119. As bound, this is actually subsumed in a reprint title, *The Sermons of Charles F. Parham* (New York: Garland Publishing, 1985), which also presents another of his books, *A Voice Crying in the Wilderness*. Each of the two books retains its original pagination.

But in theology, as in war, the losers don't get the last word and they certainly don't write the histories. The "winners," Durham's spiritual heirs — the Assemblies of God, the Foursquare Church, and others — all continue to pay tribute to Durham as the spiritual and theological innovator and father of their belief system regarding sanctification. Once they clearly won the field of battle, they became more magnanimous toward their second-blessing brethren, and the issue now seems to garner little interest, except perhaps among historians. For the majority of Pentecostals, the three-step *ordo salutis* is dead, replaced by Durham's two-step approach.

Why did Durham and his followers (who are in the vast majority today) prevail? We can adduce at least three reasons:

1. Durham had a powerful persona and a persuasive public ministry. All first-hand accounts indicate as much. His meetings were exciting, his preaching was electric, people sensed the presence of God, seekers received the Baptism in the Holy Spirit, and people got healed. The feeling was, "If this teaching

isn't correct, why is God blessing this ministry?" and it was a fair question to ask.[40]

2. As Pentecost spread, it encompassed many more people from non-holiness backgrounds than it did those of the Wesley tradition. As Assembly of God Bible scholar and historian William H. Menzies points out:

> A problem began to manifest itself in the ranks of the early Pentecostal movement when large numbers of people began to enter the movement from groups who knew neither the Wesleyan nor the Keswickian type of holiness doctrine. Most of these seem to have come from the Baptists. The Baptists generally held to a Reformed view of sanctification, in which the great emphasis was upon process, not crisis.[41]

(You may recall that, prior to his earlier, initial acceptance of "second work of grace" Wesleyan holiness, Durham, too, had been a Baptist.) These Spirit-baptized Baptists had

---

40 To be completely fair to Durham, this situation allows his camp equal rights to the argument "the God who answers by fire, let Him be God."

41 Menzies, "Non-Wesleyan Origins," pp. 90-91.

no knowledge of a need to figure out how to accommodate second-blessing sanctification into their theological framework, so they had no problem giving Durham a theological thumbs-up. The Holy Spirit seemed to see no impediment in their ignorance of the doctrine — He baptized them and gave them the gift of tongues anyway.

3. Durham was partly right. Everything pertaining to salvation *is* part of Christ's finished work. The Pentecostals from holiness backgrounds couldn't from Scripture support the caricature of the Wesleyan position that had evolved among its shriller proponents. Inadvertently, they set up their own straw men, and Durham knocked them down. That's not to say that the experience of sanctification can't be a later event, for millions have testified to precisely that "second work of grace" over the centuries. Indeed, Durham allows for this:

> Concerning experiences, *we would say that we do not doubt that many people come into conscious possession of the experience of sanctification after conversion;* but because they were not taught the truth in the first place, shall we teach

all others that they must seek sanctification as a second work?[42]

As stated above, some do not know, at first, enough of the truth to get the joy that they would receive, did they possess a knowledge of the truth. Therefore, ***with new light on what they have in Christ, comes new blessing.***[43] [emphases mine in each example]

So Durham never says that subsequent sanctification experiences aren't valid, but he insists that it needn't be experienced that way, that is, that delayed experience can't be doctrinalized. If he used terminology a bit more familiar to us, he would say that these believers merely appropriated what was already theirs in Christ.

---

42 William Durham, *Articles Written by Pastor W. H. Durham Taken from Pentecostal Testimony*, (n.p., n.d.), p. 18. This particular book seems to have been issued posthumously. The rhetoric has been toned down to a remarkable degree.

43 Durham, *Articles*, p. 19.

The Rejected Blessing

True Heirs?

STRANGE TO SAY, the one tribute Durham's spiritual heirs don't pay him is to believe a key element of his sanctification doctrine, and that key element is — *eradication!* "Durham," insists Menzies, "rejected their Wesleyan concept of eradication as unscriptural."[44] By the time Myer Pearlman, that very able Assemblies of God theologian of a bygone generation, wrote his classic theology, he, as a spiritual heir of Durham, felt he could list "Eradication of 'inbred' sin" under "Erroneous Views of Sanctification."[45]

Yet Durham claimed quite the opposite! I am indebted to Farkas for pointing this out: "...the Finished Work doctrine was not faithfully transmitted after Durham's death."[46] Farkas argues that on one level, Wesleyan holiness can be broken down to two elements, *subsequence* (i.e., the sanctification

---

44 Menzies, "Non-Wesleyan Origins," p. 91.

45 Myer Pearlman, *Knowing the Doctrines of the Bible* (Springfield, MO: Gospel Publishing House, 1937), p. 257.

46 Farkas, *William H. Durham*, p. 186.

event happens at some point in time after regeneration) and *eradication* (by which is meant that the sin nature is removed). Farkas argues that Durham's vehemence was directed only at the *subsequence*, not the *eradication*, or the deliverance from inbred sin.[47] We have already heard Durham thunder against subsequence, claiming that sanctification happens at the instant of regeneration — all at once with forgiveness, new birth, and justification. But listen to Durham himself on eradication, that is, the freedom from indwelling sin:

> ...has a man who is in Christ any sin in him? *No. It could not be.* We do not come into Christ with the "old man" in us.[48]

> When a man is convrted [sic] *he is made pure and holy*, and he has a really holy love in his heart for God and man.[49]

> *We believe that God's standard is entire sanctification*, and that this being the case no man can be jutsified [sic] in an experience short of it.[50]

---

47 Farkas, *William H. Durham*, pp. 237-238.

48 William H. Durham, "The Finished Work of Calvary," in *Pentecostal Testimony*, Vol. 2, No. 1 [Jan.? 1912], p. 2.

49 Durham, *Articles*, p. 4.

50 Durham, *Articles*, p. 27.

The old man is full of sin and ***the new man is free from sin.***[51] [emphases mine]

Referring to Romans 6:6,[52] Durham affirms,

...in other words, our 'old man,' the Adamic nature, was crucified with Christ ***that it might be destroyed or done away.***[53] [emphasis mine]

Speaking of "second work of grace" holiness people, Durham does not doubt the veracity of the inward work they claimed, for he shared the experience of a pure heart with them:

...many of ***these dear people love the truth concerning holiness, and doubtless had pure hearts...they taught real holiness of heart***, and

---

51 Durham, *Articles*, p. 28.

52 Remember, Durham would most likely have been using the King James Version, which renders the passage like this: "Knowing this, that our old man is crucified with him, **that the body of sin might be destroyed**, that henceforth we should not serve sin."

53 Durham, *Articles*, p. 17. As Farkas points out, "destroyed" was John Wesley's position as well. In a letter to his friend Joseph Benson, Wesley states, "I use the word 'destroyed,' because St. Paul does: 'Suspended' I cannot find in my Bible." (This is quoted from Letter 455 in *Letters from the Reverend John Wesley to Various Persons*; a part of *The Works of John Wesley: Addresses, Essays, and Letters*, electronic ed. [Albany, OR: Ages Software, 2000].) The *destruction* or *eradication* of sin in the heart is at the core of both men's messages.

that is what the Scriptures teach, **and that is what we believe.**[54]

...some of them...will say...that the writer [that is, Durham himself] has gone back on sanctification. **The writer is wholly sanctified to God in Christ.**[55] [emphases mine]

Durham stated clearly that his problem was not with entire sanctification — freedom from indwelling sin—but with the teaching that it was a "second work." He himself claimed to believe in and walk in entire sanctification as his personal experience:

I have always found great difficulty harmonizing the definite second work of grace theory with the plain teaching in the Word. *I had no trouble, however, in proving that the Bible taught entire sanctification. It seems to me that no one could believe the Bible and attempt to deny that its standard of teaching is Holiness unto the Lord.* But the minds of some have become so biased by the erroneous second work theory, *that you can state clearly to them that you do believe in entire sanctification and that the Bible teaches it as God's only standard* and that therefore no one can be justified short of it, and while still claiming their sec-

---

54 Durham, *Articles*, p. 30.

55 Durham, *Articles*, p. 43.

ond work experience, they will go away and say that you do not believe in sanctification.[56] [emphases mine]

Therefore there is a remarkable difference in substance between Durham and those who claim to be his spiritual progeny. Durham believed in entire sanctification — the elimination of indwelling sin — and his "heirs" do not! On the other hand, although Durham vociferously disagreed with his "second work of grace" opponents about the *timing* of entire sanctification, he agreed with them on the *substance* of their teaching — a pure heart free from indwelling sin.

What happened then, that those who adopted Durham's teaching did not adopt this key element? Probably the short answer is that Durham died while the controversy was still hot; he was cut short before he could define his doctrine more fully. Durham's followers,[57] many with Baptist back-

---

56 Durham, *Articles*, pp. 15-16.

57 One thinks of Frank Ewart, Durham's designated successor in Los Angeles. Ewart, who came from a strongly Baptist background, dealt another splitting blow to the already-fractured Pentecostal Movement as he championed the Oneness/Jesus-Only Movement. This new schism occurred just one year after Durham's death. One also thinks of Eudorus Bell, another Durham associate, who had been a Baptist pastor in Texas. Bell was the first chairman of the Assemblies of God, a Pente-

grounds, were taken up with the crusade against subsequence and (lacking the previous exposure to Wesleyan holiness that Durham had in his background) they misapplied the same zeal to eradication. To put it in the vernacular, Durham wished to throw out what he considered to be the "bath water" of subsequence, but he very much loved the "baby" of eradication; his followers, far less clear on the distinction because of their Baptist background (or perhaps with other agendas not now known), threw out the baby with the bath water. Farkas seems to favor the idea that Durham's designated successor, Frank Ewart, may lie at the heart of re-interpreting Durham's teaching:

> [Ewart] credited Durham with "supplanting" the second work doctrine by teaching sanctification as "a progressive work in the development of Christian graces in the character of the believer," and as "the gradual abandonment to the will of God," a view Ewart claimed he himself had been taught as a Baptist.[58]

It seems fitting to let Farkas bring our consideration of the Finished Work controversy to its ironic conclusion:

---

costal denomination that was founded a mere two years after Durham's death.

58   Farkas, *William H. Durham*, p. 264.

Within nascent Pentecostalism the controversy was precipitated by William H. Durham, who proposed a rival view of sanctification to the modified Wesleyan view held by virtually all Pentecostals. The dispute evoked by the Finished Work doctrine quickly became the grounds on which the Pentecostals broke apart and realigned themselves into new alliances.

Very early in the realignment process, however, Durham died, and his Finished Work doctrine was left to his successors who either fundamentally misunderstood the teaching, or intentionally altered it under the conditions prevailing at the height of the raucous controversy. As it turned out, *the original perfectionist version of the Finished Work teaching essentially went to the grave with Durham.*[59] [emphasis mine]

However the misrepresentation of Durham's doctrine happened, the truth of Entire Sanctification—that is eradication, freedom from indwelling sin—was from that time lost to the majority of Pentecostals, those who had come from non-holiness backgrounds. Durham's mission (executed with heat and fervor and a seeming lack of brotherly love and tact) was to re-focus the truth of entire sanctification onto its Scriptural basis—the finished

---

59 Farkas, *William H. Durham*, pp. 309-310.

work of Christ, not a man-made timeframe. His followers, not understanding the true goal, eliminated the heart—indeed, one might fairly say the *pure heart*—of the Pentecostal Movement's holiness underpinning.

As a result, the Cherished Doctrine, the handmaiden, the teaching that was used of God to prepare tens of thousands of hearts for the great Azusa Street outpouring—that doctrine of Entire Sanctification—was cast out and is missing. It is no wonder, then, that most Pentecostals and charismatics have never encountered her. Without her, there is a vital element from Azusa Street's spiritual foundation that is lost.

Jesus said, "Blessed are the pure in heart, for they shall see God" (Matthew 5:8). The author of the Epistle to the Hebrews echoed Jesus' words, writing of "holiness, without which no man shall see the Lord" (Hebrews 12:14). The children of the Holiness Movement of the late 1800s, who believed God for pure, sin-free hearts, saw God move in a new way at Azusa Street. The Holy Spirit manifested His end-time Pentecostal power in hearts He Himself had cleansed from indwelling sin. If God desired to bestow on our generation another move as mighty as Azusa Street, would our hearts be as prepared and pure as those of William Seymour and his co-workers? Or would God's gift of Entire Sanctification suffer continuing exile as the Rejected Blessing?

The Rejected Blessing

Epilogue

Epilogue

A Word to My Pentecostal and Charismatic Brethren (Eavesdroppers Welcome!)

I WILL LEAVE YOU TO PONDER a Scripture with which you are probably familiar, but perhaps you will come to see it in a different light. You will know of the great Jerusalem Council in Acts 15, which the Church convened to learn of God's work among the Gentiles and to determine how those same Gentiles should fit into God's economy. Luke paints a realistic picture of the council starting off with "much disputing" (v. 7).

At a certain point, Peter stands up to share, and the Holy Spirit has Luke record exactly what he shared (vv. 7-11), because he was speaking under the inspiration of the Spirit. Remember, now, that this is the same Peter who was there at the Day of Pentecost (Acts 2) and did the public preaching under the revelation of the Holy Spirit. This is the same Peter used of God to break down the barriers to the Gentiles when he was bidden of the Holy Spirit to speak at the home of an officer of the Roman army of occupation, a man we all know as Centurion Cornelius (Acts 10). God did remarkable things on those two great days in Church history — people were saved, baptized in the Holy Spirit, and they spoke in tongues.

At this Jerusalem Council Peter harks back to those two experiences of "a good while ago," pointing out that the Gentiles' experience was every bit as Divine as that of the original Pentecost band. He even draws on the most striking parallel he can to prove his point, and if you are a "tongues as initial evidence" person, this may surprise you. Hear the great Apostle:

> And God, which knoweth the hearts, bare them witness, giving them the Holy Ghost, even as he did unto us; And put no difference between *us* and *them, [fill in the blank]*.

I've left the rest of verse 9 blank. Can you fill in the blank from memory?

1. Did Peter say, "God... put no difference between us and them—they all got saved like
we did"? Well, they *did* get saved, obviously,
or there wouldn't have been a "Gentile
issue"—and most of you wouldn't be reading
this, and I wouldn't be writing this. But, no,
Peter had something else in mind.

2. Did Peter say, "God...put no difference between us and them — they all spoke in
tongues just like we did on the Day of Pentecost"? That would have been a very "Pentecostal" thing to say, and it's certainly true
that Cornelius' household, family, friends,
and house guests *did* speak with tongues
(10:46).[60] But, again, no — Peter's words
avoid the obvious and outward.

In fact, avoiding the *outward* and concentrating
on the *inward* is how Peter starts his comparison
statement. Let's read the passage again with the
blank filled in:

---

60 Just to set the record straight, by God's grace I, too, have received and enjoy the gift of speaking in tongues, along with
the gift of interpretation of tongues. I don't say that as a boast,
as it's not my doing. But I didn't want my Pentecostal brethren
to get the idea that I am disparaging that wonderfully edifying
and Scriptural gift.

> *And God,* **which knoweth the hearts,**[61]
> *bare them witness,*
> *giving them the Holy Ghost,*
> *even as He did unto us;*
> *And put no difference between us and them,*
> **purifying their hearts by faith.**
> *Acts 15:8-9*

That was it for Peter, the God-given "sign" that proved to the great preacher of Pentecost that the Gentiles had "got it": their hearts were purified by faith. They had been sanctified! Yes, they were saved — glory to Jesus! In the power of the Spirit they miraculously spoke in tongues — how wonderful! But all those years after the Day of Pentecost, to bolster his argument and make his case as strong as he could in the council, Peter's testimony was that God gave those Gentiles *the Spirit's witness of purified hearts.*[62] Entire sanctification —

---

61 Here Peter alludes to that famous verse about the wickedness of the human heart, Jeremiah 17:9-10—"The heart is deceitful above all things, and desperately wicked: **who can know it? I the LORD** search the heart..." This starting point in Acts 15:8 sets up a very interesting contrast with Peter's conclusion in verse 9.

62 And let us note, in passing, that this also corresponds to what God spoke to Peter in his rooftop vision: "What God hath cleansed, *that* call not thou common" (Acts 10:15). Of course, at the time of the vision, Peter thought God was talking about

heart purity — rather than tongues, was Peter's standard of comparison! The *Holy* Spirit had made them *holy.*

As the centennial of Azusa Street draws near and we contemplate Pentecostalism's second century, we would do well to earnestly and prayerfully consider Peter's Spirit-inspired declaration. Does God have something wonderful in store for us — cleansed hearts, free from inbred sin? Our Pentecostal forefathers, those in the first, fresh wave of the 20th-century outpouring, believed He did, and they knew that it was a key element in a world-shaking revival. God again poured out His *Holy* Spirit into *holy* hearts. It seems that even the man who rocked the early Pentecostal world with his opposition to the movement's initial position on sanctification was not opposed to the teaching of freedom from inbred sin; he only argued the *when*, not the *if*, of heart purity.

As we look back to God's sovereign outpouring at Azusa Street, we need to bear in mind the words of the Prophet Isaiah:

> *Listen to me, you who pursue righteousness,*
> *Who seek the LORD:*

---

unkosher food and unclean animals, but, in retrospect, Peter came to see that God was talking about *cleansed hearts!*

> *Look to the rock from which you were hewn,*
> *And to the quarry from which you were dug.*
> *Isaiah 51:1 NASB*

If we look to that "rock" and "quarry" of Azusa Street from which all modern-day Pentecostal and charismatic experience has been "hewn," we will rediscover our missing heritage and re-embrace the rejected blessing, the heart-cleansing key that opens the door to "old time Holy Ghost power" — Entire Sanctification.[63]

---

63 Three steps, two steps—or one step? Before Durham, the Pentecostal Movement taught a three-step process from salvation through sanctification to the Baptism in the Holy Spirit. Durham, by insisting that justification and sanctification were part of the same instantaneous event, reduced the process to two steps. An irony seems to appear when we study the reports of the event at the house of Cornelius as it is reported in Acts 10, 11, and 15—there was only one step! Cornelius and company, the first Gentiles ushered into God's Kingdom, received salvation, sanctification, and the Holy Spirit with no intervening steps! Even the most-reasoned (or most argued!) theology may be made to appear foolish next to the wisdom of God.

Bibliography,
Index,
and Other
Matters of Interest

Bibliography

(Partially Annotated)

Barrett, David J. and Todd M. Johnson. *World Christian Trends AD 30 - AD 2200: Interpreting the Annual Christian Megacensus*. Pasadena, CA: William J. Carey Library, 2001.

Bartleman, Frank. *Another Wave Rolls In* (formerly, *What Really Happened at Azusa Street*), edited by John Walker, revised and enlarged edition; Monroeville, PA: Whitaker Books, 1962.

_____. *Witness to Pentecost: The Life of Frank Bartleman*. New York: Garland Publishing, 1985. This reprint edition actually includes four Bartleman titles: *From Plow to Pulpit, From Maine to California*; *How Pentecost Came to Los Angeles*; *Around the World by Faith: Six Weeks in the Holy Land*; and *Two Years Mission Work in Europe Just before the World War, 1912-1914*.

Burgess, Stanley M., ed. and Eduard M. Van Der Moss, assoc. ed. *The New International Dictionary of Pentecostal and Charismatic Movements*. Grand Rapids, MI: Zondervan, 2002.

Blumhofer, Edith Waldvogel. *The Assemblies of God: A Popular History.* Springfield, MO: Radiant Books (Gospel Publishing House), 1985.

_____ and Grant Wacker. "Who Edited the Azusa Mission's *Apostolic Faith*?" in *Assemblies of God Heritage*, Vol. 21, No. 2, Summer 2001. (No, the mystery editor's name isn't here. Keep reading...)

Durham, William H. *Articles Written by Pastor W. H. Durham Taken from Pentecostal Testimony.* n.p., n.d.

_____. *The Pentecostal Testimony.* Various issues, including (I believe) all of the complete extant issues: Vol. 1, Nos. 5 (July 1, 1910) and 8 (1911?); Vol. 2, Nos. 1 (January 1912?), 2 (May? 1912), and 3 (July?/August? 1912—this is the memorial issue).

Farkas, Thomas George. *William H. Durham and the Sanctification Controversy in Early American Pentecostalism, 1906-1916.* Doctoral dissertation, The Southern Baptist Seminary, 1993.

Goff, James R. *Fields White unto Harvest: Charles F. Parham and the Missionary Origins of Pentecostalism.* Fayetteville, AR: The University of Arkansas Press, 1988.

Gohr, Glenn. "The Finished Work" in *Pentecostal Evangel*, May 31, 1998 (No. 4386), pp. 10-

11.

Harper, Michael. *As at the Beginning: The Twentieth Century Pentecostal Revival.* Plainfield, NJ: Logos International, 1965.

Martin, Larry. *In the Beginning: Readings on the Origins of the Twentieth Century Pentecostal Revival and the Birth of the Pentecostal Church of God.* Duncan, OK: Christian Life Books, 1994.

_____. *The Life and Ministry of William J. Seymour and a History of the Azusa Street Revival.* Volume 1 in the series *The Complete Azusa Street Library;* Joplin, MO: Christian Life Books, 1999. The author's treatment of Durham in this book is grittier than his chapter in *In the Beginning.* Martin's indexing is very helpful, but, oh, that this book had a bibliography!

Menzies, William W. "The Non-Wesleyan Origins of the Pentecostal Movement," pp. 81-98 in *Aspects of Pentecostal-Charismatic Origins*, Vinson Synan, ed.; Plainfield, NJ: Logos International, 1975.

Parham, Charles F. *The Everlasting Gospel.* (n.p., n.d), p. 119. As bound, this is actually subsumed in a reprint title, *The Sermons of Charles F. Parham* (New York: Garland Publishing, 1985) which also presents another of his books, *A Voice Crying in the Wilderness*. Each of the two books retains its separate pagination.

Parham, Sarah E. *The Life of Charles E. Parham, Founder of the Apostolic Faith Movement*. New York: Garland Publishing, Inc., 1985. This is a reprint of the original, which appeared in 1930. It could be a very helpful tool if it had an index.

Pearlman, Myer. *Knowing the Doctrines of the Bible*. Springfield, MO: Gospel Publishing House, 1937.

Seymour, William J. *The Azusa Street Papers: A Reprint of The Apostolic Faith Mission Publications*, Los Angeles, California (1906-1908). Foley, AL: Together in the Harvest Publications, 1997. (It is more likely that Clara Lum *should* be listed as the real editor of Azusa Street's *The Apostolic Faith* publication, but for simplicity's sake, we will credit Seymour; it serves her right for absconding with the mailing lists!)

_____. *The Doctrines and Disciplines of the Azusa Street Apostolic Faith Mission of Los Angeles, California*. Larry Martin, ed.. This is Vol. 7 in Martin's series *The Complete Azusa Street Library*. Joplin, MO: Christian

Life Books, 2000.

Synan, Vinson, ed. *Aspects of Pentecostal-Charismatic Origins*. Plainfield, NJ: Logos International, 1975.

_____. *In the Latter Days: The Outpouring of the Holy Spirit in the Twentieth Century*. Fairfax, VA: Xulon Press, 2001.

_____. *The Century of the Holy Spirit: 100 Years of Pentecostal and Charismatic Renewal, 1901-2001*. Nashville, TN: Thomas Nelson Publishers, 2001.

_____. *The Holiness-Pentecostal Tradition: Charismatic Movements in the Twentieth Century*. Grand Rapids, MI: William B. Eerdmans Publishing Company, 1997.

Wacker, Grant. *Heaven Below: Early Pentecostals and American Culture*. Cambridge, MA: Harvard University Press, 2001.

Wesley, John. Sermon 89: "The More Excellent Way," in *The Works of John Wesley: Sermons*. Electronic edition; Albany, OR: Ages Software, 2000.

Index

Apostolic Faith Gospel Mission (see Azusa Street Mission)......................................22

Apostolic Faith, The (newspaper). 22, 23, 26, 28, 30, 31, 39

Azusa Street Mission......................................22

Bartleman, Frank......................................40

Bell, Eudorus......................................55

Durham, William......10, 16, 27-30, 32-40, 42, 43, 45-49, 51-57

Ewart, Frank......................................56

Farkas, Thomas......................29, 51, 52, 56

North Avenue Mission (Chicago)..............10, 30

Parham, Charles..................5-8, 30, 31, 41, 42, 45

Parham, Sarah......................................43

Pearlman, Myer......................................51

Pentecostal Testimony (newspaper)...33, 34, 37, 39, 40, 49

Seymour, Jenny Moore......................................29

Seymour, William..........7-9, 25, 29-31, 35-37, 39

Wesley, John......................................16

The Rejected Blessing

About the Author

THROUGH OVER FOUR DECADES of pastoring, writing, and teaching at home and abroad, Jim Kerwin's calling and credentials as a gifted Bible teacher have been established in the hearts of his growing audience. In the unique tapestry of his ministry can be found influential threads from early Methodism, Wesleyan holiness, and the Pentecostal and charismatic movements. Dedicated to "rightly dividing" the divinely inspired Scripture of truth, and to faithfully presenting God and His truth to his listeners, Jim's goal is to always minister in "the Spirit of wisdom and revelation in the knowledge of Him" (Ephesians 1:17). Jim holds a Master's degree in Biblical studies from Regent University's School of Divinity.

Jim is the founder and president of Finest of the Wheat Teaching Fellowship, a ministry that focuses its resources on "teaching God's text, in context, without pretext," with a special emphasis on training pastors and leaders in developing countries. Many of Jim's Bible-teaching articles and audios appear on the **FinestOfTheWheat.org** website. In addition, he hosts the *Kernels of Wheat Podcast* on the **KernelsOfWheat.com** website, where his blog posts also appear. As the conservator of the works of his mentor, P.H.P. ("Percy") Gutteridge, Jim issues the monthly *Grains from Gutteridge Podcast,* as well as occasional Gutteridge articles from transcripts.

Books from
Finest of the Wheat

The Rejected Blessing by Jim Kerwin (also available in
   e-book format for Amazon Kindle, Barnes & Noble
   Nook, and Kobo e-book readers)
   (KernelsOfWheat.com/books#trb)

That Uncomfortable Word—Conviction! by Jim Ker-
   win (available in e-book format for Amazon Kindle,
   Barnes & Noble Nook, and Kobo e-book readers)
   (KernelsOfWheat.com/books#conviction)

Faith Is Substance by Percy Gutteridge, edited and
   annotated by Jim and Denise Kerwin
   (KernelsOfWheat.com/faith)

Boyhood Memories and Lessons by Isaiah Reid, compiled, edited, and annotated by Jim Kerwin
   (KernelsOfWheat.com/boyhood)

**Sunnyside Papers: Inspirational Sketches from God's
   "Book of Nature"** by Isaiah Reid, compiled, edited,
   and annotated by Jim and Denise Kerwin
   (KernelsOfWheat.com/sunnyside)